Alley

Written by Jill Eggleton
Illustrated by Trevor Pye

The alley cats lived
in shadowy places.
At night they came out
for food.

They went . . .

Darting down the alley,
darting down the street,
and drum, drum, drum,
went their alley cat feet.
Alley cat feet,
alley cat feet,
moving to the rhythm
of the alley cat beat!

The alley cats saw a bin
by the butcher's shop.
"Food," they howled . . .

and they scratched on the bin
with their alley cat paws.
Scritch, scritch, scratch
went their alley cat claws!

There was
such a commotion
and a hullabaloo
that the people
in the street shouted,
"**Shoo, cats, shoo!**"

So off went the alley cats!

Darting down the alley,
darting down the street,
and drum, drum, drum,
went their alley cat feet.
Alley cat feet,
alley cat feet,
moving to the rhythm
of the alley cat beat!

The alley cats saw a box
by the fish shop.
"Food," they howled . . .

and they scratched on the box
with their alley cat paws.
Scritch, scritch, scratch
went their alley cat claws!

There was
such a commotion
and a hullabaloo
that the people
in the street shouted,
"**Shoo, cats, shoo!**"

So off went the alley cats!

Darting down the alley,
darting down the street,
and drum, drum, drum,
went their alley cat feet.
Alley cat feet,
alley cat feet,
moving to the rhythm
of the alley cat beat!

The alley cats
saw the baker's shop.
Pizza smells squeezed out
from cracks in the walls . . .

so they scratched on the door
with their alley cat paws.
Scritch, scritch, scratch
went their alley cat claws!

There was
such a commotion
and a hullabaloo
that the baker
opened the door.

In rushed the alley cats.
They darted over boxes.
They darted over bins.

Alley cat feet,
alley cat feet,
moving to the rhythm
of the alley cat beat!

"**STOP!**" shouted the baker.
"**I can't have cats
in my shop!**"

But the alley cats
wouldn't stop.

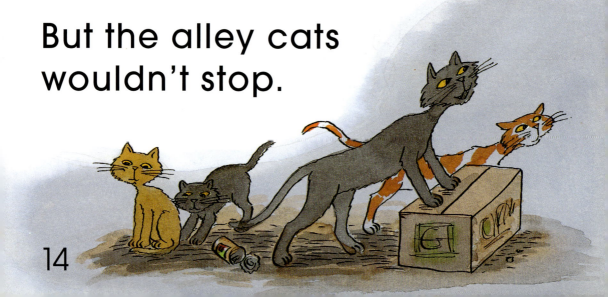

The alley cats saw
some gigantic bins.
"Food," they howled,
and they leapt right in.

Flour puffed out,
like smoke,
all over the baker's shop.

"**Fire! Fire!**" shouted the people in the street. "**There's a fire in the baker's shop!**" And they called the firefighters.

But when the firefighters looked in the baker's shop, all they saw was . . .

. . . a white, white baker chasing floury white cats!

"Come on, alley cats,"
said the firefighters.
"We will give you food!"

"Food!" howled the alley cats.
"Jump on the fire truck!"

Riding down the alley,
riding down the street,
and drum, drum, drum,
went their alley cat feet.
Alley cat feet,
alley cat feet,
moving to the rhythm
of the alley cat beat!

Guide Notes

Title: Alley Cats
Stage: Year 3

Genre: Fiction
Approach: Shared Reading
Processes: Thinking Critically, Exploring Language, Processing Information
Written and Visual Focus: Change of text style

THINKING CRITICALLY
(sample questions)
- What do you think this story could be about?
- What do you know about alley cats?
- How do you think cats become alley cats?
- Why do you think the alley cats come out at night?
- What do you think the alley cats might do the next night?
- Could this story be true? Why/Why not?

EXPLORING LANGUAGE

Terminology
Title, cover, illustrations, author, illustrator

Vocabulary
Interest words: darting, shadowy, rhythm, commotion, hullabaloo, scritch, floury
Compound words: firefighters
Contractions: can't, wouldn't
Singular/Plurals: shop/shops, bridge/bridges, cat/cats, firefighter/firefighters
Antonym: day/night
Homonym: their/there
Synonyms: commotion/hullabaloo, scritch/scratch, muttered/mumbled
Simile: 'puffed out like smoke'

Print Conventions
Capital letter for sentence beginnings and names, full stops, exclamation marks, quotation marks, commas, question marks, ellipses, apostrophes